Only the Strong Can Survive

-ALEJA BENNETT-

PublishAmerica
Baltimore

© 2005 by Aleja Bennett.
All rights reserved. No part of this book may be reproduced, stored in a retrieval system or transmitted in any form or by any means without the prior written permission of the publishers, except by a reviewer who may quote brief passages in a review to be printed in a newspaper, magazine or journal.

First printing

At the specific preference of the author, PublishAmerica allowed this work to remain exactly as the author intended, verbatim, without editorial input.

ISBN: 1-4137-9237-5
PUBLISHED BY PUBLISHAMERICA, LLLP
www.publishamerica.com
Baltimore

Printed in the United States of America

Table of Contents

INTRODUCTION	5
Being Alive	7
Escaping the Fire	8
Silent'ness Within	9
Survivor	10
Your Eyes	11
Why me	12
A Forgotten Romance	13
A Little Girl Scared	14
Abandoned	15
All Races Unite	16
Brighter Days	17
Broken Hearted #1	18
Broken Hearted #2	19
Childless	20
Faith	21
Fatherless	22
Forgiving	23
Ghetto	24
Grace	25
Helping Yourself	26
How to Make It	27
Hungriness	28
I'm Not A Quitter	29
I'm Only Human	30
I'm Strong	31
Insanity Has No Place Here	32
It Was All a Dream	33
Let's Live	34
Locked Out	35
Longing	36
Loneliness	37
Looking Out the Window	38
Love	39
Motherless	40

Neither Black or White	41
Not you're ordinary Woman	42
Only the Strong Can Survive	43
Patience—-Positive Choices	44
Powerful	45
Powerless	46
Prison	47
Racism	48
Rest	49
Sensual Feelings	50
Striving For A Cause	51
Suicidal	52
Wise Decisions	53
Yes We Die	54
You Are Fantastic	55
You Crossed The Line	56
Innocent	57
Being Lied On	58
Doors being Shut	59
Feeling Angry	60
Flashbacks	61
Holding A Grudge	62
Homeless Not Being Respected	63
Homelessness	64
No Stopping Us	65
Not being believed	66
People Thinking You're Crazy	67
Regret	68
Thinking about giving up	69
To 2 Unwanted Mother's I Made It #1	70
Wanting To Scream	71
A Forgotten Romance	72
I'm Only Human	73
To Two Unwanted Mothers (My short story as an abused adopted child)	74
Not your Ordinary Woman	78
Special Thanks To You All.	79

INTRODUCTION

Hi, my name is Aleja;
    I do hope that you are enthused about my life in poetry form. *Only the Strong Can Survive* is about my life and life itself. These poems were written at the time I needed to forgive and heal. Adoption is supposed to be a special thing but for me it wasn't. For the rest of my life I will have to live with all the memories of being abused. With the unknown knowing of my biological parents and siblings, I will continue my search. Upon adoption I was told that my mother does not want to be found, truly that was another sad day for me adding on with many others. Praying to God that one day my heart will find the peace it's looking for. Through the years many people have come into my life and supported me. A few men came into my life and disappointed, lie, and played with my emotions. They knew all about my life and still made the wounds deeper and deeper. Truly I know that this woman that stands today is strong. This is a book for all ages to understand. My next book coming soon will be Seasons with and without Love, also in poetry form. May God bless and keep you all in his tender care. What we all must face in life during the events only the strong will survive.

A special thanks to PublishAmerica for giving me this chance and seeing in my work what no one has seen.

Being Alive

To me, being alive you can accomplish a lot
and no one can tell you that you cannot.

Being alive you can be whatever you want to be.
It's all up to you, when you decide you'll see.

You will make mistakes, this you will do
but when you learn from it you can start a new.

Being alive all starts from being a baby
and when we grow up we'll be a man or a lady.

Some of us have been abused and even used by people that are cruel.
They think we are some kind of freaking fool.

Being alive, people hurt us over and over again
but we mess up when we let them win.

We may drink and get high to erase or not think about our past
but you're only hurting yourself just like other people have.
Be strong and go on and live your life.
Don't go on forever carrying hate.

Don't let pain eat you up inside because one day it can be too late.
Being alive is a wonderful thing,
and when you choose life you'll be on top of everything.

Escaping The Fire

So you've been through the fire
For life you still have a desire
You are a person I do admire
following the pattern sticks and stones
You came out with no broken bones
your tears poured as it burned
Life is one lesson to be learned
A cry for help you yearned
During the flames, patience and
virtue you have earned
listening to the talented dangerous liar
you untangled the deadly wire
while doing this you've escaped the fire.

Silentness Within

Deciding to keep it buried
I was a little child worried
To my rescue no one hurried
All those secrets kept for years
The pillow absorbed all of my tears
trembling at night with childhood fears
no one to run and tell
On my knees to God I fell
pretty eyes of mine would swell
only to God I gave a quiet yell
burying all the sadness
why was i going through such madness
I wasn't doing any childhood badness
No one helped me back then
knowing where and when
the secret silent"ness kept within.

Survivor

Survived I have and always will
Pain we go through in life is real
knock downs and bruises
mean people have such good excuses
From let downs to being put down
Still I remain in this awful town
Being beat even a needle stuck in my feet
This kind of behavior is not sweet
but see, I refuse to let history repeat
I've been knocked down
but guess what I'm up again
See you lost and I win.

Your Eyes

Sparkles that so glitterly shine
Your warm hand embraces mine
Giving off a feeling of ginger wine
your eyes, your eyes
how bright to mines they shine
uplifting receiving a sensuous feeling
daydreaming yet quite heart warming
glossy as a fine glass of wine
hypnotizing underneath a rainbows shine
come hither precious pearls
escape me to an unknown world
fill me with extreme passion
eyes of purity fashion
long gevity is what Im asking
your eyes gives me complete satisfaction

Why Me?

You are chosen to be the best
Different, unique, and wiser than the rest.
You've made it through life's hardest test
whatever you need accomplished go for it
slow down take your time you're worth it
clear your mind and set it free.
This will help you be the best you can be
Writing, singing, or acting
whatever it may be let it become long lasting
You can achieve to greater heights
not looking back at what your life was likeYou can say
I'm free!I'm free! I'm free!
no, it couldn't be
why me? honestly,why not me?

A Forgotten Romance

A never taken stroll
To hands too distant to hold.
Yearning for that being wanted
thirsty, hungry, never even noticed.
Sensual intimacy unseen
emotions trapped inside this human being.
Life with you was unexplored
The want was simply ignored.
Most treasured moments deepen
Awake, at the lake or sleeping
memories of a touch kept creeping.
Releasing yourself away from me
No time to see how good it can be
You relieved me from this misery
hopes, dreams, fantacies are history.
sadened you have left my inner soul
free for anothers hand to hold
No hate. Just lonliness.
And this,
A wish for romance.

A Little Girl Scared

Only if these walls could talk
Why don't angry people take a walk.
My body is nervous and shaking
poor little hands can't stop trembling.
Stop thinking Im hearing impaired
Im just lonely and scared.
hearing the belt hit against the wall
for no apparent reason at all.
Things were done just to make me scared
A hurting child and no one cared.
My father always made me jump
punching my head always giving me a lump.
Having to take off all my clothes
horribly taking all those blows.
still nobody even knows
but see, Im not scared anymore
being scared is not what I
was put on this earth for.

Abandoned

You left me all alone
leaving me with no
mom to call my own.
My nights were lonely and sad
Even wondered sometimes about my dad
was it me you wish that
you never had.
abandoned, neglected and mistreated
With my children it wont be repeated
knowing what it's like to be
constantly beated.
Oh mom why, did you give me up?
never listening, always telling
me to just shutup.
Through all this and more
I have grown up
Leaving my heart numb and torn up.

All races Unite

Just because we have different
shades of color, simply doesn't
mean we shouldn't love each other
let's stop the hate people
by coming together.
The separation has me a bit worried
Don't you know that one day we will
all be buried. While alive
lets make peace or start to like
each other atleast.
black is beautiful, white is adorable,
racism is terrible, killing between
the two is unbearable.
Wrong, right, black or white
All races let's unite.

Faith

Something you hoped for
could be standing at the door.
the evidence of what you can't see
One day it will be.
What ever you cant see with your eyes
may one day be an awaited surprise.
rushing for something can lead to nothing
wanting consists of waiting
waiting turns to be longing
you find waiting to be very boring.
If you believe
there is no doubt that you will achieve
Once you achieve will you believe?
In life we must learn to wait
Your destiny is never too late
Just have a little faith.

Fatherless

So you had a drug addiction
Did you know my adoption was
years of affliction.
You turned your back on me daddy
living your life as free as can be
someone was always hurting me
this went on as a child constantly
not being able to tell anybody.
I know you had a problem
maybe you tried to solve them.
I also was addicted to something
The alcohol made me feel
like nothing
The pain, the hurt was still there
Until my parentless feelings
I began to share.

Forgiving

Holding this all in and not forgiving
will never help me to really start living
it happened, now its over
besides I've become older.
I have to let this go,
Forgiving at one time was flat out no!
Now its just not so
The hands of time can't go back
Even though I deserve some of that.
Don't we all wish this
alot of happiness we had to miss.
People will always do wrong
It amazes them when you come out strong
Forgiving is what we should have
done all along.

Ghetto

Ghetto mentality
come to reality
you think your speech is normal
whats wrong with talking formal
Yo Yo word up to me is abnormal
The way you speak expresses your
character by talking ghetto
doesn't make you a master
why impress people on the street?
If you don't will they
think you are weak? Will you
find a beautiful woman by
saying Yo shorty? after that
lets go to my crib
and get naughty, Do you
know how to rise? Open your
mouth and talk wise she
then will look into your eyes
ghetto language will fill
her with disgust and anguish.

Grace

Tender heart be a little patient
around the corner good things are waiting.
mind be free of negative activity
humanity be aware of your sensitivity
let strength, honesty be apart of me
An open mind along with setting past hurts and abuse free.
I need a little more of you
To get passed what Im going through.
When I am feeling weak
Enter my mind softly to speak
being chosen, humble and meek.
Consecrate and guide my feet
To walk in the paths of good forune to meet
I want to be a little more sweet
Just as my appearance is neat
All I need is a little more grace
That I may live with this human race
As I travel all over the place
Add to me my higher power, more grace.

Helping Yourself

Employ yourself, respect yourself
appreciate yourself, love yourself
Don't worry about anybody else
forgive yourself, clean up yourself
Don't regret yourself, be yourself
temporarily forget about everybody else
take control of yourself
Then look at yourself
This is all apart of helping yourself.

How To Make It

A push and a goal to keep I have
who cares if people choose to laugh
someone greater is working on my behalf.
The storms may continue to rise
people may never even apologize.
But I must hold my head up high
this I'll do until the day I die
You may even ask me why.
It's because I feel that I can make it
I'm too talented to let my life be wasted.
No matter how big the blows
I will follow life's positive arrows
and maybe hey who knows
just maybe I'll be one of those
famous heroes.

Hungriness

My hungriness is for life's fullness.
I want a taste of its richness
achieving my goals
touching other souls
reaching out my hand for
someone to hold
keeping homeless people
out of the cold
my writing and things
that I do will be positive.
I don't have any time for the
negative with this world
I have to be up to speed
wanting to know who is
really in need
there's no room for bitterness.
My hungriness
Is for a life of blissfullness.

Im Not A Quitter

Fairwell I say to giving up
saying hello to you no matter what.
Losers is for users
users is for abusers
abusers are pathological liars
liars should have their tongues
cut out with pliers.
A quitter is not a winner
the winner is a survivor
this survivor will continue
to go higher, from higher to wiser
then wiser will make them stronger
when stronger you'll live longer
living longer makes you a winner
Not A QUITTER.

Im Only Human

Bones with wet flesh looking at what society is doing,
I'm only human.
Veins, blood going through a stream
cutting this will make me scream.
Oh world of a killing machine,
What are you doing? I'm only human.
My waist is sliming fast
with grace I just might last,
being such a demon, forgetting
I'm only human. Skin that soon will peel
A heart which one day will heal
being human I'm real I feel.
God of all understandings
search me with wonderful findings.
Soften my heart yet harden this body
Give me a tasteful life like candy.
Through fighting the war, winning the race
taking my rightful place
towards heaven to enter in,
yes world, I made it by being only human.

Im Strong

I am simply genuine
healthy, intelligent and fine
buildings can fall
I'll still stand tall.
waves may smother me
No ocean will drown me
there's no room for
self pity
Not in this big city,
My goals keep me busy
as I put on my dress
looking my best
I'll sing a beautiful song
even wear a thong
Whatever I decide to do
I as woman am strong.

Insanity Has No Place Here

Insanity, stay far from me
From the depths of hardships
energy blow on me.
Coming at me are strong winds
of the mighty sea.
Dig me out of this cave
Im sweltering,
Inner soul full of love
Is melting.
reasssure a need to stay calm
it's not of me to cause pain
suffering or bodily harm
Higher Power add to my soul
strength with peace.
Clean, restore, direct my brain
Allow me to maintain
because someone is trying
to drive me insane.

It Was All A Dream

Cooking, cleaning, talking
loving, yet I was dreaming.
Laughing, smiling, driving
hugging, romancing,
still just daydreaming.
sexing, screaming, longing,
humping, the sweating,
past hurts forgetting
I only was dreaming.
wanting, touching, grabbing holding,
only for a moment
It was over, I was dreaming.
Deep kissing, breath taking,
heart pounding, fingers strolling,
Still I was dreaming.
Farewell, goodbye
From beginning to ending
I was only, with eyes open
Dreaming.

Let's Live

As we all know we only live one life.
Those of us alive know what life is like
Why are we so easy to give up?
Is this what your dreams are made of?
if you want to really live
It's starts by trying to forgive
then your mind is clear and free
you're on your way to being
the best you can be
everyone that knows you will see.
Do all the things you enjoy
possibly can afford
Go buy yourself a Honda Accord
Take a trip, don't waste time being bored.
Loving is wonderfully living
and living is achieving.

Locked Out

Shattered broken dreams
It's more worse than it seems.
Where will I go?
What about tomorrow?
Oh how and when will I be fed
wanting to feel the warmth of a bed
open doors has to be ahead.
closed houses are all around me
Now Im starting to feel lonely
as if Im in this cold world only.
Yeah, Im locked out
without a shadow of a doubt
Is this what life is about
If so I am now finding out.

Longing

Anticipated, frustrated
beated, mistreated
still nobody I've hated
but I patiently waited.
yearning, needing
dreaming, praying
caring and always sharing
but I still kept loving
A mother is what Im longing
Wanting to feel that belonging
So I can continue to keep singing
this for me life is not bringing
forever my soul will continue
to be longing.

Loneliness

Silently I slowly drift
time so rapidly went
false friends had my money spent
all along my heart was broken and bent.
My eyes hardly closed for sleep
Alot of nights I would just weep
trusting no one with secrets I keep.
The darkness of lonliness
filled me with such sadness
reminding me of all the badness.
but,one glad day
the lonely stone rolled away
Knowing now, it;s gonna be o.k.
Now I say thanks to the
Lord for another day.

Looking Out The Window

Sometimes I often look out my window
through it I can see my shadow.
I look at the people passing by
Sometimes I even wave and say Hi.
Looking out your window you'll
see alot of things. Trees, people,
blue sky and the beauty it brings.
im grateful for the beauty I can see
next time my lover will be with me.
then we can enjoy looking out
the window together
moments I will cherish forever
If we don't do it again ever in life
We did it once, next time maybe
I will be his wife
Then we'll be sleeping together every night
Back to the window fantasizing
what this would be like
adorable, beautiful just like the sky
wonderful.

Love

Oh love, only you I"ll forever think of
sweet, hot, passionate deep love.
As my toes curl
I drift off to another world.
this is so exciting
When you're not around Im fantascising.
Soft touches from your hand makes
me weak, exhaustion from your love
rocks me to sleep.
Oh love, don't ever depart
If this happens It'll break my heart
Our love is like an art
beautiful, different and lovely
my dear I love you only
Until the day I lay in my grave
from the sky to you I'll wave
This is what most precious
dreams are made of—LOVE.

Motherless

There is a missing void
life sometimes feel totally destroyed.
No tight warm hugs
not even a single bed time tuck
No taking me to the park
My childhood felt lonely and dark.
I was surrounded by so much anger
feeling, my life was in danger.
sitting in corners all alone
hearing the sounds of a loud tone.
it was so disastress
being motherless
I always dreamed of you mother
even while I was beaten by the other
You don't know the hell I was under
My childhood was like rain and thunder
You left me motherless
but Im still here never the less.

Neither Black Or White

Why must we be a color
Why not respect each other
If Im not the color of your skin
Does it mean I lose, you win
being homeless would you let me in?
No color is better than the other
We all must live together.
You'll see each other in
a restaurant, maybe not what you want.
There's good and bad in every race
City, State, Continent, any place
For each of us there is space
We are all part of this human race.
Black, white, don't choose to fight
Let us all wake up
and come to the shining light.

Not Your Ordinary Woman

Im not your ordinary woman
precise to the point
living like a queen
is what Im doing
Im not your ordinary woman
style, class, bodily oils
carefree personality
polite behavior is my inner doing
Im not your ordinary woman
giving not receiving
bringing calmness to the earth
focused on goals to be achieving
loving, full of passion
eternal friends yours for the taking.
Im not your ordinary woman
no make up, just plain
my ways are always the same
unique has my name.
Loving me not, such people are doing
Respect that, Im not your ordinary woman.

Only The Strong Can Survive

In life we go through many things
facing it and the heartache it brings
sometimes we're not on top of things.
eventually we start to rise above it all
somebody helped us up as we started to fall
There was no one you had to call
you felt stuck against the wall.
Don't stay there move away
be confident in yourself each day
telling yourself it'll be o.k.
maybe it wasn't so bad after all
now that you're standing straight and tall
go out treat yourself and have a ball
only the weak ones give into giving up
they feel as if they have no luck
it's not luck you're just blessed
separated, being different from the rest
you have survived the world's hardest test
You gave positive action your best.
Only the strong will be able to carry on.

Patience

Positive assurance
release my endurance.
positive arrow
let me folllow the straight
not the narrow.
conscience be my guide
help me to swallow my pride
standing strong through the tide.
I find that patience is a virtue
it's not always easy to do.
feelings slow down and wait
Rapid heart beat slow down your rate
You see, patience helps you to wait
The word is not ancient
It's everyday patience.

Positive Choices

Bring some cheer my way
Maybe I'll have a brighter day.
I need your advice to be good
Don't leave me burning inside like wood.
my foot is moving forward
How come you're moving backwards?
Your negative energy is simply
no good for me. When you decide to
help yourself, leaving behind
everybody else, it will awake you
te reality, time waits for nobody.
Find yourself surrounded in positive
situations, positive voices
Most of all positive choices.

Powerful

I am fearless
with an open awareness
achieving that I am different
painfully acceptig how my childhood went
now being able to pay my own rent
standing up tall
after a knowck and a fall
I wanted death to be my call
leaning and crying against the wall
Right now I am a huge success
everything that I do is done with my best
No more looking sad and pitiful
but feeling strong and incredible
nomore feeling so sorrowful
because today I am powerful

Powerless

Rise up against this demon
Free the things that you're dreaming.
An addiction does make you powerless
You've found yourself in alot of mess
Having this weakness, you're careless.
Of life you seem to have a fear
You must get it together my dear.
being down in the dumps isn't pleasant
I know because for me it wasn't
taste lifes richness and fullness
get rid of your lifes dullness.
You're too blessed, to be powerless.

Prison

Through these bars and this chain
im still trying to maintain.
awful things happened that I want to tell
No one will help me when I scream or yell.
Why am I in this prison?
I made the wrong decisions
wishing to my mother I had listened
Now Im in jail and it's her I missing
Im away from home and very far
ther's no escaping this, not even with a car
It will not get me too far
You have to be here to know what
prisons are
I want to go home but
instead I can only use the phone.

Racism

Can we stop the hate of color
Why is it so hard to love each other?
Blacks had a terrible past with the whites
Now, no one wants to come
together and unite
Instead we just want to fight
For the kids is this right?
We make them hate with all our might
Blacks and whites you need to see the light.
Let's bury the past
people are dying too fast
How long will this last?
We don't need racism
Just some positive criticism.

Rest

This load I carry is so heavy
my feelings are starting to be weary.
Oh trials and tribulations stay far
See, now I know who people really are.
My heart needs a break
There's no more that I can take
only wanting now to rest
being put through lifes hardest tests
having no mother to lay upon her breast
To this hard life I need a rest.
evil doers always get by
loving everybody is what I try
even when people start to lie.
I wish I was far out west
In my own little nest
so i can finally start to rest.

Sensual Feelings

Hold, mold, feel
thrill and tease me.
Stimulate, motivate
excite and resuscitate.
Move, enthuse, create
gently massage me.
fullfill, keep it real
that chill, I feel
man you move me.
emotions run wild
your style, that smile
brings out that child
inside of me.
lovely, funny
my easter bunny
my true one and only.

Striving For A Cause

Alright the billows rolled
lies has started to unfold
I was thrown in the cold
My terrible childhood story
was on hold, Now guess what?
No Im no where near old.
Im striving for a cause
I may even have some flaws
Don't we all?
It's not their call.
My destiny is totally up to me
years of searching, here it is finally,
my long awaited quest
only desiring to be the best
please excuse me while I pause

Because Im striving for a cause.

Suicidal

Quitting is what Im thinking
sorrow's what Im feeling
enemies is what Im reaping
It now must come to an ending.
My eyes are always red
There are people I even dred
The word love no one has said
maybe Im better off dead.
Why stay here so unhappy?
Nothing right now makes me happy.
The devil whispers death in my ear
There must be a reason why Im here.
Maybe I'll stay to achieve something
Instead of dying accomplishing nothing.
To the evil spirit of suicidal
Trying to snuff me out
like a reptile
Guess what?
Im going to be here
for a while.

Wise Decisions

Your choice was very wise
What is the need to apologize?
some people need to open their eyes
Does pride have so much size?
Regretting mistakes we make
try learning from them, it was just
a mistake, No, life is not a piece
of cake. Being wise is knowledge
For this you don't need college.
get down from the fence
Just use your own common sense.
In your very own eyes
One day to your surprise
You will find that your own
new decisions have become wise.

Yes We Die

We're here for a short little while
Don't wear a frown, put on a smile
Look forward to one day walking
down the isle, if you have a desire
Don't throw it away in the fire.
Is there something you never did?
Maybe you want to have a kid
Life is just like a closed lid
Open it so you can breathe and live.
Living reminds me of a bird, free,
flying, rememberings you've heard.
To me, life is like a train that
comes back, when it does you are
on the right track
Yes we all have to die
why waste time asking why?
Live to the fullest just don't try
If we do this we will be ready to
say goodbye, when the precious
Lord calls us to die.

You Are Fantastic

Carry a warm embrace
A smile on your face
Along with a little grace
believing life is not a waste.
Your kindest words brighten
someones day.
Goodmorning, How are you?
Have a pleasant day
people notice you're fantastic
right away.
you're addicted to being different
You have a beautiful characteristic
your unique talent is very artistic
This makes you to be fantastic.

You Crossed The Line

Playing me like a fool
Toying me like a tool
messing with my mind
yeah, you crossed the line!
Telling me all kinds of lies
using your sick twisted alibyes
your butt should be mine!
Oh yeah, you crossed the line!
Stealing my finest valuables
listening to your constant troubles
with you is like I was seeing doubles.
I listen to you constantly wine
hell yeah, you done crossed the line!
Stealing my lover man
with my heart in your hand,
you still seem not to understand
for me the sun will always shine
but baby, get to stepping
You've crossed the line!

Innocent

No wrongness I have done!
Im not the only one!
Why am I not beleived?
there's no one that I've deceived.
Will I pay for a crime I didn't comitt
How will i deal with it?
In this world we are blamed for things
What's sad is the pain it brings.
Innocent—jail time spent
Innocent—away from paying your rent
Innocent—where has your lawyer went
Innocent—I was struck and hit
Innocent—No one wants to hear it
Innocent—I was robbed, all my money spent
Innocent—guilty has become my verdict
Innocent—I swear to it
I didn't do it
Because Im innocent.

Being Lied On

I didn't do what you said I did
after all I was just a little kid
How much can I possibly do?
Knowing what I would have to go through.
Stop telling peole that Im crazy
You are the ones that are dizzy.
Making up lies on me because of what you do
All these years you thought no one knew.
See, the lies that you often tell
will send you straight to a burning hell
No parole or time in jail, just hell!
I sure felt like I was there, especially
when I had to take off my underwear
that wet greasy belt my skin it would tear
Always being naked and bear.
Liars, Liars, if you can hear
Come out, Come out
where ever you are!

Doors Being Shut

Alright this door was shut
Now this one too but so what.
The same door you slambed on me
will be the same one you open
for being hungry and thirsty
I will be there to give you some
water or hot tea. You see,
we never know who we will need
And whose mouth you will have to feed.
The person you closed the door on
Do you remember saying that you wish
that they were not born?
Too bad you had to toot your own horn
While watching someones life be torn.

Feeling Angry

Tearing down these walls
pleading for someone to hear my calls.
Strong towers knock me to my knees
wont somebody stop what's going on please.
Feelings are about to explode
hidden secrets are about to be told
untruths unravel and unfold
Childhood treatment was brutal and cold
Feeling like for pennies I was sold.
Fists punching my little swollen lips
stroking my skin with wet whips.
A powerful kick to my side
swallowing the pain with pride
keeping these awful, unbearable pains
all trapped inside
For years you've covered up and lied
releasing all of this anger
simply puts no one in harmful danger.

Flashbacks

Flashing my painful past across my face
making me feel like my lifes a terrible waste
while streams of tears roll down my face.
Why did this awfullness happen to me?
Flasbacks!! Why not let me be?!!
these painful memories, you struck me
with so suddenly, half of it I told nobody
All I want is to be set free.
How do I come out of
what I was just reminded of?
Ah yes, my one true inspiring love
If not the special wonder from above
Being known as God and his never changing
love.

Holding A Grudge

Sometimes I wanted you to pay
terrible things to me you would say
See, you knew it hurt right away
sticking the knife deep day after day.
I use to hold a grudge against you
because of the awful things you would do.
Not beleiving that I made it through
Now my plans are positive and new.
Hidden darkness comes to the clear light
You will see your wrongness wasn't right
destroying me with all your might.
My little face to you was an always
annoying sight. This grudge that I
held is no more, letting go and feeling
a free happiness is what I aim for
All the grudges has walked out the door
To never haunt me anymore.

Homeless Not Being Respected

Why are we not respected? Every comment
or word we are being pushed away, rejected.
Don't professionals know we have pain
We are all not the same
Not even the same name
Being homeless is not a game
Unpolite words workers say should be ashamed.
Puerto rican, white, red or black
We must stand up and be strong
See, we wont be homeless for too long
With patience, grace we'll carry on
Let's ignore their comments and weather this storm.
Every smiling face is not nice
We get pushed away once then twice.
Why can't a homeless person be positive
Please, stop making us become negative.
Being that we have just one life to live
Don't take away from the homeless instead
give. Considerastion, nice words, patient
Help us along so time isn't wasted.

Homelessness

So, you threw me to the streets
pregnant, alone, scared feeling weak
abortion, you told me to seek
When you said this I couldn't
even utter words to speak.
The streets wasn't going to be my home.
Im sure starting to feel all alone
No family, close friends or mom to
call on the telephone.
I can do this and will make it on my own.
Some way, somehow, Im not giving up
Oh where, Oh where, is my luck?
My stomach is feeling so empty
Does my family even feel guilty?
Wont someone have some pity
Im homeless in this lonely dark city
Will somebody, anybody, please help me!!

No Stopping Us

Marching, marching moving forwardly ahead
Justice, justice, let the truth be said
Homeless people and the poor must be fed
No more of our people shall be dead!!
While listening and praying
This race we stay in.
walking forward not backwards
making sure our points are understood.
Free at last, free at last
part of the present not the past.
Ringing out freedom
In the world we live in.
In God we trust, with that
There's no stopping us!

Not Being Believed

You both enjoyed doing this to me
even other people can see.
Slaps, kicks, punches, along with
the dirty looks. All that time
you started to believe your own lies
even your sick twisted alibis.
other people believed your untrues
While I sit back with the blues.
No one believes that you hurt me,
then why did I often cry so suddenly?
It hurt when no one believed me
As I sat in my bedroom looking so sadly
wanting someone to believe me badly
If they did I would and still would
appreciate it gladly.

People Thinking You're Crazy

There's nothing else you can think about me
Telling me Im lazy but Im too far from being
crazy. Watch out on whom you call this
maybe education, you took a miss
They couldn't read so it was you that they
decided to diss. With your smartness and
brains, this drove them insane
You were suppose to be crazy but you felt
nothing for years but pain
everyday of your life was like rain
Your whole family treated you the same.
Now take a look at you, all that you've
even gone through. Notice that you are still
standing straight and tall, what happened
to you didn't make you fall, listen, after
all life is up to you. It is your call
To get up, fail or to fall.

Regret

Remembering past actions of myself
never revealing to anyone else.
Now I have to live through it
By starting over becoming the worlds greatest poet,
thats right and I sure do know it. My regret enables
me to show it. Finally picking
up the missing pieces
one day collecting my riches
Oh regret, don't leave me in stitches.
mean people often bring it up
Like they have finally grown up.
My regret wont let me forget
moving on it wont let me yet
Stand in my way? try me let's bet.
Im constantly moving on
leaving my regrets where they belong
This I'll do as years prolong
Soon those regrets I felt will all be gone.

Thinking About Giving Up?

Winds blow, the rain may continue to fall
God is sitting patiently for you to call
he knows you're being drived up the wall.
Let the tears flow, you think he doesn't
know. Look at the beautiful rainbow,
glance at the pretty whit fallen snow.
What about the trees, flyng by you
can see the stinging bumble bees.
All the food you're blessed to eat
maybe you want something sweet,
look at your legs, arms and feet.
Listen to your voice, you're not
here by choice but here for a wonderful
reason. Don't give it up in this season
Only yourself and God you should be pleasing
Still thinking about giving up?
Whats the reason?

To 2 Unwanted Mothers, "I Made It"!
#1

One abandoned me
then another totured, abused
and lied on me. No pity.
Always feeling so lonely
No one around to ever hold me.
from the age of nine there are memories
tears, blood, hot tub water, no other kids
I was the only adoped daughter.
Given the gift of singing, reading
reciting and writing, it kept me living.
Yes, I was beaten, tossed to the side
sitting in corners until one day
I would not take it any longer
Those bad things helped me to become
stronger to wiser from wiser to kinder
from kinder to always looking higher
from lower back up to higher
I may fall but eventually stand up
no one wanted me when I was down
So, don't want me when I become rich.

Wanting To Scream

Screams stay away at this moment
It would just bring more torment
screams I beg you to be silent
If you don't someone will be violent.
Screams just wait a little longer
For me you have to be stronger
You coming out will make me a goner.
Screams be quiet, I tell you!
sheding tears quietly, we can do
Let's make a wish for it to come true
maybe no more pain for us to go through.
Still wanting to scream
No, just be silent, me and you
knowing it's not an easy thing to do.

A Forgotten Romance

A never taken stroll
To hands too distant to hold.
Yearning, for that being wanted
thirsty, hungry, never even noticed.
Sensual intimacy unseen
emotions trapped inside this human being.
Life with you was unexplored
The want was simply ignored.
Most treasured moments deepen
Awake, at the lake or sleeping
memories of a touch kept creeping.
Releasing yourself away from me
No time to see how good it can be
You releived me from this misery
My hopes, dreams, fantacies are history.
Sadened you have left my inner soul
free for another's hand to hold
No hate, Just lonliness,
and this,
A wish for romance.

I'm Only Human

Bones with wet flesh looking at what
society is doing, I'm only human.
Veins, blood going through a stream
cutting this will make me scream
Oh world of a killing machine
what are you doing, I'm only human.
My waist is sliming fast
with grace I just might last
being such a demon, forgetting
I'm only human. Skin that soon will peel
A heart which one day will heal
being human, I'm real I feel.
God of all understandings
search me with wonderful findings.
Soften my heart yet harden this body
Give me a tasteful life like candy.
Through fighting the war, winning the race
taking my rightful place
towards heaven to enter in
Yes world I made it by being only human.

To 2 Unwanted Mothers
(my short story as an abused adopted child)

One abandoned me,
then another tortured, abused,
lied on me, no pity.
Always feeling so sad and lonely
Is there someone around to even hold me.
The age of nine are hurtful memories
tears, blood, hot tub water, bloody lips,
Hot comb dragging through my scalp,
My mother's foot on my little neck,
A vacuum cord cutting open my hand,
A swift kick to the edge of a sharp glass table,
My little side hurt for two weeks straight.
Thinking every day I was going to die.
Being fed whenever she felt like feeding me.
While in the hot scolding water she beat me with
A bathroom plunger. Every Saturday I was forced
To eat eggs even though they knew I didn't like them.
If I threw it up I had to swallow it back up. When I threw
Up my father gave me swollen bloody lips with his fist.
To this day I remember looking in the mirror as the tears
Flowed looking at my swollen lips, back to the table to
Finish the rest of the eggs they had for me to eat until
They were all gone. These people had no remorse for
Me what so ever. Every Saturday was torcher. Saturday
Night my mother would drag a hot comb through my
Scalp and kept doing it every time I cried. When she
Got to my edges she burned them too. If I screamed
She would hit me in the head with that hot comb fresh
Off the stove and I could do nothing but pray that she would
Not beat me with it anywhere else. If I did not know my
Sunday school lesson from word to word I would have to
Stand on one foot until my feet and legs were numb. Can I sit

Down now? No!!!!! I felt like an abused slave well dressed
Cinderella on Sundays and Monday through Saturday in a cage.
My father loved punching me across the head and punching me in
My lips outside of church just for talking to the other kids.I never
Missed a Sunday. No matter if I was sick or not I had to go until
I finally got thrown in the streets at 19 for becoming pregnant.
The worst thing I ever had to do was lick my own urine off the
Floor. I asked if I could use the bathroom while sitting on the
Floor in front of her in the gold and black chair. She told me to
Sit there and finish my homework. Ma, I have to pee real bad
Please let me go. She still aid no and the pee starting coming down
Right to the floor and she said you better lick it all up, right now and
I did because I was so scared of them. My father watched as I licked
Up my own piss off the floor. I got beat with wet belts, extension cords,
Sticks, golf clubs, switches, vacuum cords, plungers, hot combs, umbrellas,
Fists, feet, even when I was five she stuck a sewing needle in my foot to
See if I was awake. I faked as If I was sleep so they wouldn't bother me.
If she thought I told something she had the hot sauce sandwiches ready
For me with no water to drink. My mouth burned like hell and that kept
Me quiet because if I talked my mouth would burn with hot sauce and as
Many times as she desired. To this day I still have the marks and the nail
Dent o the right of my face where she poked me with her nail and left me
With a dent for life. My life as a kid was a fashion show and I was the well
Dressed kid on the block and people think I had it all but the clothes was
Their covering and my own room was their covering also. I wasn't ready
To be on my own at nineteen but I had to and I struggled ever since with no
Support from my adoptive family. Now that I'm in my thirty's, I have moved
On and only by the grace of God I am alive today. I chose the wrong men to
Love me because I wanted to be loved now I am by myself for two years and it
Feels good to no longer allow people to use and abuse me anymore.
Given the gift of singing, reading,
reciting, writing, it kept me living.
Yes, I was beaten, tossed to the side
anger beneath the tears I cried.
Where are you mother? hello
are you out there, have you died?
Why don't the both of you love me?

Am I really that sad looking and ugly?
No, I am beautiful
My skills are meaningful
To you both, my living is now wonderful!

Not Your Ordinary Woman #2

I'm not your ordinary woman
precise to the point
living like a black queen
is what I'm doing.
I'm not your ordinary woman
carefree personality,
poilite behavior is my inner doing.
I'm not your ordinary woman
no make up, just plain,
my ways are always the same,
unique has my name,
on my way to fortune and fame.
Being this black woman I maintain,
I rain, I pain, once slain,
driven almost insane,
sometimes this life's a strain,
but I still remain,
to be not you ordinary woman.

Grace and peace be unto you and my God bless and keep you all in a very special way. I've survived abuse and anyone can too, Don't feel sorry for me but instead rejoice because I'm a survivor. When my mother and father forsake me then the Lord will take me up. To all the people I admire, this is a special and warm thank you. Victory Missionary Baptist Church, Barbara Raieny, Gussie Coates, Cora Jordan, Marcia Jamerson, Mae Newsome, Tamika Waller, Moses Herring, Mrs. Anderson, Sylvia and Rudy Sumpter, Karen Jackson, Flo Coates, and her family, Nicole, Tiffany, and to Roy may you rest in peace. Rabaza, Estelle, and also a special and warm thank you to Pastor Gatling for being there for me when I needed him and always having a listening ear. I love and always will love the entire church as a whole Victory Baptist Church. I want you all to know that out of sight does not mean out of mine, you all alre always in my thoughts and one day I will be coming back home to stay. A special thanks also to the Rhema Sanctuary of praise which is located in the Bronx. Thank you all for loving and supporting me through my entire pregnancy. Momma and Poppa Sylcott, Thanks for letting me be your daughter and feeding my pregnant belly. To the whole church thank you all for your financial contributions, when I had nothing. You all are appreciated in a very special way, I will always love you all. To my adopted parents thanks for not loving me because while you were not there and not loving me God was loving me all along and he sent his angels to protect me from hurt harm and danger. I have become a strong woman thanks to you and I did not write this to hurt anyone but for me to heal and if I can heal all the abuse children and adopted children all around the world. If I had one question for my adopted parents it would be, Why did you do it to me? Why don't you both love me unconditionally like you love your blood family? If I don't receive an answer it is ok because I have gotten on with my life and I hold no grudges because God takes care of it all. In the end only the strong can survive. If I didn't write your name don't hold it against me it is too many I love you all once again.

    I would like to add the Richmond Hill Library in queens for all their help also a special thanks to Edna Velasquez for all her help in assisting me in the making of my book and also to Jenera Burton for her on going help and giving me as much time needed on the computer to finish the making of Only The Strong can survive. To you all I am extremely grateful and to my new found love from the Caribbean of Jamaica Chris Sinclair, I do love you very much and i thank you for your encouragement, loyalty, honesty and asking me to be your wife this is a special thanks to you my dear I have waited so long to find you and i thank you for coming into my life and helping me to be strong through what ever I have to face in life. To my wonderful children Arthea, Shamel and Jessica I love you all more than you know and no matter what mommy will always love you all the same and as high as the rivers and as large as the mountains. To Tamika Waller I would like to thank you for the years of putting up with me and just being there for me when no one was. You fed me and my children and took me in when we were homeless and as you stated I was the house guest from hell. The person that never wanted to leave. You were there for all those nights I cried and the times I was drunk and broke your tub handle (laugh). I love you very much Tamika and I will never forget you. To Barbara Rainey you are another one who has done the same as Tamika and for this I am truly grateful. When my adopted parents didn't take me in you did until i got on my feet and I want you to know I love you so much and thanks for listening when I needed to talk. Aunt Scrappy you are the greatest to me, you would never see me hungry and I love you very much.

```
811 Bennett
Bennett, Aleja.           JUL 2 4 2007

Only the strong can
  survive /
        c2005.
```

NO LONGER PROPERTY OF
THE QUEENS LIBRARY.
SALE OF THIS ITEM
SUPPORTED THE LIBRARY

Printed in the United States
48463LVS00004B/57

9 781413 792379